Thatched Ireland

Dedicated to Norma Smurfit, without whom this project
would never have materialised.

This edition published 1995 by
John Hinde Limited, Dublin 18, Ireland.
under licence from The Ugly Duckling Co. Limited.

Paintings by Róisín O'Shea © Róisín O'Shea 1995
This edition © Róisín O'Shea 1995
Text © The Ugly Duckling Co. Limited.
Edited by Donald Sutherland and Róisín O'Shea.

Acknowledgments:
Caitriona Foley and Marie Mulligan,
research assistants.

An Artists Portfolio

Thatched Ireland

A Collection of Pen & Ink & Watercolour
paintings by Irish artist Róisín O'Shea.

Born in Cork, Ireland in 1960, Róisín O'Shea studied at the National College of Art and Design, Dublin, and following graduation headed to Sydney, Australia, where she completed a post-graduate diploma in the City Art Institute. On her return in 1985 she continued painting, drawing her inspiration from her native landscape which continues to captivate her today. In her 19 years of painting Róisín has built up an enormous collection of sketches, paintings and photographs from the length and breadth of Ireland which led to this series of books.

INTRODUCTION

Almost every visitor I have encountered in Ireland associates thatched cottages with the essence of Irishness. Abroad, the image that most commonly portrays Ireland is again the thatch. A friend of mine from New Jersey, Maureen, asked me some time ago why I did not paint thatched cottages; so I started to look for this part of Ireland that I had somehow only seen in terms of decay or ruin, having painted derelict cottages again and again, each deserted building telling me more about Irish history in emotional terms than anything I had ever read. In researching this book I was amazed to find so many well-kept thatched buildings hidden all over Ireland, in particular the village of Kilmore in County Wexford, which has an astonishing number of thatched cottages along the seafront. It surprised me that most of the thatches were being lived in year round and maintained with a sense of pride. It gives me great satisfaction to see this craft alive and well in Ireland today – I had somehow relegated it to times gone by. This volume contains a collection of the buildings that I found on my first extensive trip around Ireland.

Róisín O'Shea

SMALL WATER PUMP, BUNRATTY VILLAGE

This type of pump was the most efficient way to get fresh water from the deep, natural, man-made wells.

BUNRATTY, LIMERICK

Within the grounds of Bunratty Castle lies Bunratty Folk Park. This charming village is an exact recreation of a typical Irish village at the end of the last century. The variety of dwellings range from pubs to farmhouses to traditional work areas of blacksmith and printer. The cottages can be admired with their fully furnished interiors, complete with old style fireplaces.

CROOM, LIMERICK

Sadly, since I first painted this cottage the lady of the house has passed away. Her son, a bachelor, now lives in the cottage and although his gardening skills are not up to those of his mother, this is still a beautiful building with its steeply pitched roof with hipped ends and sliding sash windows.

ADARE, LIMERICK

Estate villages were becoming quite common in the early 19th century. These cottages were built in 1830 by the Third Earl of Dunraven, who resided in Adare Manor. The appearance of these estate villages improved greatly when the landlords were made responsible for their workers. Accommodation usually comprised kitchen, a parlour and one or two bedrooms, set in half an acre. The cottages depicted in the painting are more in keeping with a picturesque English village, the designs for which usually came from pattern books based on the English Tudor style.

DOOLIN, CLARE

These cottages with their bright, cheerful colours are hard to miss in the small village of Doolin. They have been put to good authentic use as shops and a restaurant, still maintaining their appeal as thatched cottages.

DERELICT, CLARE

This derelict cottage caught my eye as a sad reminder of all those people who were forced to leave their homes through hardship, often emigrating with the title deeds of their property which meant that no one could restore or redevelop these buildings. They remain as ruined testimony to the thousands who never came back.

'BALES FOR SALE', CLARE

Until 1800, hay was not widely used since livestock were not housed and fed during the winter due to the mild climate. To stop hay rotting in the damp climate it was left in small round bundles, with a hole in the middle to let the rain run off. The hole let the hay dry fairly quickly. By the end of the 19th century, haymaking was much more popular and had become increasingly mechanised.

THATCHER AT WORK, CLARE

For the most part local materials were used, hence the ease with which the different type of thatch fits into the surrounding countryside. Thatching skills were passed on from generation to generation; sadly, less than ten true working thatchers exist in Ireland today.

GAP OF DUNLOE, KERRY

This cottage about 8kms from Killarney, is surrounded by spectacular scenery. This famous 6km gap goes through the MacGillycuddy's Reeks mountain range in County Kerry. Local people say that the summer evenings are the best time to take in the scenery, and ponies can be hired to make the trip. Unfortunately, every time I have visited the Gap it has been pouring rain, so I could never see further than Kate Kearney's Cottage!

TEACH SIAMSA, KERRY

A well-built thatched cottage, Teach Siamsa is located in Finuge, County Kerry. It is one of the National Folk Theatre rural training workshops, where young people in training present a show on the traditional folk ways and customs of the area each Wednesday evening during July and August. Unfortunately, I got there on a Tuesday!

THATCH PUB
KILLEAGH, CORK
This beautiful thatched pub is located on
the main Cork road to Dungarvan.

MALAHIDE, DUBLIN
This cottage is set in the old seaside town of Malahide. This neat
little cottage is an example of the reason why Malahide has been
the recipient of several Tidy Towns Awards.

Roisin O'Shea

THATCH AND HAYSTACK

The type of thatching material has changed over the years, with straw thatch now harder to replace due to modern harvesting methods and new strains of wheat with short stems. Some roofs, depending on the climate, are heavily roped with stones or attached to pegs built into the wall. A variety of material is used - reeds, bracken, etc.

SWISS COTTAGE, TIPPERARY

Named after its obvious resemblance to an alpine chalet, the Swiss Cottage was built in 1810 as a gentleman's residence for Richard Butler, Lord Cahir. It was designed by the famous architect John Nash. Marie-Antoinette, the French Queen, was largely responsible for starting the trend of building the cottage ornate, having one built in the area in front of her palace to satisfy a childish whim. The trend soon caught on and the Swiss Cottage is thought to be the best example of this style.

HIGH CROSS, KILDARE

This cottage has sadly been demolished in recent times. The local community tried its best to have it preserved, but this was not the case. This painting will at least preserve it for posterity and in the memories of those who cared about it. Many of my paintings depict the vanishing face of Ireland, as the subject matter has often been demolished to make way for more modern buildings. Hopefully the paintings will serve as a reminder of the unique and indeed beautiful architecture to be found on many of Ireland's country roads.

The sign on the post reads: HIGH CROSS INN 15 KM

SKERRIES, DUBLIN

The name comes from the rock islands which lie off its coast, Red Island, Colt Island and Inis Patrick Island. It is said that St. Patrick crossed the harbour in low tide on his way to Ulster (hence the name Inis Patrick translates to St. Patrick Island).

KILMORE QUAY, WEXFORD

Situated on the east side of Forlorn Point, this village is famed for its beauty and thatched, white-washed cottages. On my travels around Ireland I have yet to see so many thatched cottages together and indeed so many varieties. At the time that I did this painting, this house was for sale; as an artist I couldn't picture a more fitting retreat during the summer months. Hopefully I'll spend my twilight years in such a cottage I was especially taken with its unusually strong rust colour.

Cousins O'Shea.

WOMAN AND BABY'S COT, TYRONE

Cottage life has always been intrinsically linked with the hardships of famine and emigration. In 1841 the population of Ireland was over eight million, but forty years on it was estimated at barely four million. This impoverished population was almost entirely rural and survived almost solely on the potato.

BALLYGARRET, WEXFORD

This is Gerry's Farm in Ballygarret! I am sure that the gentleman carrying wood in this painting thought I was absolutely mad as I balanced precariously on top of a pillar to get a photograph. Two-storey thatched dwellings are not that common and I was never one for a wasted opportunity, even though a tall hedge obstructed my view.

RED THATCHED, GALWAY

Driving out of Galway city, I found this unusually tiny cottage surrounded by modern semi-detached buildings. It was probably a crofter's cottage which usually comprised not more than one room.

COTTAGE INTERIOR

My grandmother was an excellent cook. During my summer holidays in Kilrossanty she was always baking bread or scones or potato cakes, and the smells drove us crazy when we were kids. This cottage interior is in some part due to those memories; the women baking is my grandmother and the room is a composite of Mrs. Coffee's kitchen and my grandmother's house.

STACK OF REEDS

There are three main kinds of reeds used in thatching a roof: reeds grown in salt water, those grown in fresh water and those grown in a combination of fresh and salt water, the latter being, I am told, the best reeds to use. The average life span for thatched roofs made from the first two types of material is approximately fifteen years, whereas apparently the fresh and salt water reeds last up to thirty-five years!

THATCHED PUB, SLIGO

Originally it was a private house and was licenced in 1828 when it was a coaching inn. It has been in the family for over 300 years – the official deeds go back as far as 1828. As a coaching inn, the thatch was used as a halfway stop to refresh both people and animals on the journey to Sligo town from places such as Collooney and Dromard, in the days when this 24 to 32km trip was a strenuous journey.

WOMAN IN KITCHEN, TYRONE

The 'crane' – that most essential piece of farmhouse furnishing. Before the advent of mass-produced stoves, hearths were usually equipped with devices for suspending pots and kettles above the fire for cooking. The most simple device was a chain attached to a cross-bar in the chimney, with 'S' shaped hooks for hanging the pots at particular heights. The word crane is particularly apt, as the device was pivoted, enabling large hot, heavy pots to be swung from the fire. As such they must have been a great improvement on the simple chain.

GATE LODGE, FERMANAGH

Usually an important member of staff lived in this gate lodge. It was his or her duty to keep an eye on the passing traffic of visitors and traders. The accommodation for such a member of staff would have been deemed luxurious in comparison to their peers, as normal staff accommodation was usually very poor. When the 1881 Land Act was enacted the rights of tenants were greatly improved.

STRADBALLY, WATERFORD

As a child I spent my summers in a village called Kilrossanty. We would head to Clonea Beach or Stradbally Cove to swim. For years I gave my imagination free reign as to who lived in this cottage. I wavered between an evil sorceress or a plump, kindly godmother figure. To this day I have no idea who lives there and in all honesty I don't want to know. I can see this cottage turning up in the children's books that have been floating in my head for years.

TEA CAKE ON WINDOW

Somewhere in Ireland there is the smell of tea brack, wafting through an open window as it cools . . .

CAMPHILL COTTAGE, TYRONE

Thomas Mellon was born in Camphill cottage on February 3rd 1813. It is said that the cottage was built chiefly through the labour of his father and uncle. The cottage stood on a twenty-three acre farm subdivided from his grandfather's larger estate. At the age of five Thomas moved to America, where he worked on his father's farm in the state of Pennsylvania. Encouraged by his mother, he worked his way through college initially to become a professor of Latin. He was admitted to the Bar after studying Law. In 1870 Thomas started a small private bank known as T. Mellon and Sons. Out of this humble start evolved the present Mellon National Bank and Trust Company, one of the ten largest in the United States. Thomas Mellon died in Pittsburgh at the age of 95.

DRESSER, TYRONE

The Irish dresser is the best known of any of the range of kitchen furniture. The dresser is unique amongst the furniture of the Irish kitchen because of its primary role as an aesthetic and decorative focal point, a role simultaneously combined with the functional storage of kitchen 'ware' and utensils. Irish dressers were purposely built to display 'delph'. Until well into this century, possession of a range of domestic utensils was by no means for everyone in a society where some were so poor that they could not even afford drinking vessels. Food was often eaten directly by hand. It is not surprising, therefore, that those who did possess such 'ware' displayed it prominently.

BALLYLIFFEN, DONEGAL

This Donegal cottage is situated on the Inishowen Peninsula. This part of Ireland can be extremely bleak during the winter months and buildings usually have small windows to retain as much heat as possible from the hearth. The walls are also extremely thick and go some way towards keeping out the elements. A common feature found in a Donegal cottage is an extension which housed a double bed, positioned beside the hearth for maximum heat.

WOMAN SPINNING, TYRONE

As you go around the Ulster American Folk Park in county Tyrone, you can see re-enactments of life as it was in Ireland shortly before the famine. This woman showed how the spinning of wool was done by my ancestors.

BLOODY FORELAND, DONEGAL

The feature of this cottage that caught my eye was the extension with the blue corrugated roof. Later additions to thatched cottages were often roofed with corrugated iron as it was cheaper to maintain than thatch. Many cottages around Ireland were completely roofed with corrugated iron to keep the maintenance costs down and thereby a great deal of heat that had been trapped by the insulation of the thatch. This particular thatch has rocks weighing down the thatch to avoid it being lifted in strong winds.

INDEX